Written by Walter Wangerin Jr.

MARY'S FIRST CHRISTMAS

Illustrated by Timothy Ladwig

ZondervanPublishingHouse
A Division of HarperCollinsPublishers

Mary's First Christmas

Copyright © 1998 by Walter Wangerin Jr.

Illustrations copyright © 1998 by Timothy Ladwig

Requests for information should be addressed to:

Zondervan Publishing House

Grand Rapids, Michigan 49530

Library of Congress Cataloging-in-Publication Data

Wangerin, Walter.

Mary's first Christmas / by Walter Wangerin, Jr. : illustrated by Timothy Ladwig.

   p.   cm.

Summary: Four readings based on the Christmas narratives in the Bible in which the Blessed Virgin Mary tells her five-year-old son, Jesus, the story of His birth.

ISBN 0-310-22216-8 (hardcover : alk. paper)

1. Jesus Christ – Nativity – Juvenile literature.   2. Bible stories, English – N.T. Gospels.

3. Mary, Blessed Virgin, Saint – Juvenile literature.   [1. Jesus Christ – Nativity.

2. Bible stories – N. T.   3. Mary, Blessed Virgin, Saint.   4. Christmas.]   I. Ladwig, Tim, ill. II. Title

BT315.2.W35   1998

232.92 – DC21   97-51811

                      CIP

                      AC

Text design by Joy Chu

Printed in Mexico

98 99 00 01 02 03 04 /v DR/ 10 9 8 7 6 5 4 3 2 1

To Brittany,
who always greets me
with great cheer — W.W.

To David — T.L.

1

"*Yeshi?* Yeshi, come. It's getting dark."

A woman lights an oil lamp, then kneels and unrolls a flat mattress made of straw. The room is chilly, so she spreads a woolen blanket over the mattress.

"Yeshi," she calls, "it's time for you to sleep now."

She lays a little pillow filled with goat's hair at the top of the mattress. This is a treat, since poor people don't usually sleep with pillows. The woman's face is dark with thinking. She has something on her mind. Her name is Mary.

"Yeshi!"

Now a small boy comes into the room. His head is wrapped in a rough piece of cloth—a bandage, brown with blood. This is Mary's son. She calls him "Yeshi" as a nickname, but his real name is Jesus.

"Let's have a look at that," she says.

Mary unties the bandage. In the middle of the child's forehead is a gash, a purple wound. Mary touches it.

"Does it still hurt?" she says.

Jesus nods, his eyes big with sadness.

"I'm sorry those boys threw stones at you," his mother says. She opens a small stone jar and pours olive oil onto the tips of her fingers. Gently she rubs the oil on Jesus' forehead, to keep the bandage from sticking to the wound.

"It wasn't your fault, Yeshi," Mary says. "People can be cruel. Just after you were born, a very old man named Simeon made a prophecy about you. He said that when you grow up people will hurt you much worse than this. Ah, Yeshi!"

The woman binds the bandage around her child's head, then hugs him tightly.

"Lie down, and I will tell you a story before you sleep."

As Jesus crawls under the blanket, his mother stretches out beside him, saying, "It's a true story, a very important story. It's the story of how you were born.

"And the reason why I want to tell it to you is love. You should never forget the love. When the bad days come, you should remember that on the night you were born the whole sky exploded with love, and the angels shouted, and more than a thousand thousand hearts were in love with my baby Jesus on his birthday!"

My Love

The story starts with an angel.

Actually, it was just a plain day for me. I was hoeing in the bean patch, dreaming about the man who was going to marry me soon—Joseph the carpenter, strong and true.

But suddenly the sky went dark. I looked up and saw a great black cloud blocking the sun. It flashed with lightning, and the lightning made thunder, and the thunder seemed to be talking!

This thunder did not say, *K a - B O O M !*

Instead it said,

"Hello!"

The thunder said,

"HELLO,
YOU PERSON
PRECIOUS
TO GOD!
THE LORD
IS WITH
YOU!"

Who was the thunder talking to?

To me! Oh, that scared me.

I turned to run, but all at once the sun was
shining again, because the cloud had drawn narrow,
like a tornado, and was dropping down to the earth,
down to the bean patch, down to me!

When the tip of the long cloud touched the
ground, I looked, and in the middle of the whirling
wind I saw an angel, and the angel was talking to me,
but this time his voice sounded like breezes in the cedar
trees.

"Don't be afraid," he said. "God
has chosen you, Mary, to give birth
to a baby, a boy; and you shall call his
name Jesus."

A baby? I dropped the hoe. I almost sat down on the
beans. I was going to have a baby boy?

Just then the angel began to sing:

He will be great, and he will be called
The Son of the Highest of High;
He will be king over Israel
And his kingdom will never die.

That song was as lovely as trumpets. Birds landed on branches to listen, and the donkeys raised their ears. But I kept thinking about the baby, because the angel had made a mistake.

"Excuse me, sir," I said, "but I *can't* have a baby."

The angel frowned and blinked at me.

"Because," I said, "I don't have a husband yet."

Right away the angel grinned and began to sing again:

> The Spirit of the Highest of High
> Will overshadow you,
> And holy shall your baby be—
> God's son! And your son too.

"You see?" the angel said. "With God nothing is impossible. For example, how old is your cousin Elizabeth?"

"Old," I said, "very old."

"Well," said the angel, "in three months that woman, who never could bear a baby before, is going to become a mother. What do you think of that?"

Babies! Elizabeth and I were going to have babies—and mine would be Jesus. My baby was going to be you, Yeshi!

So I said, "Yes! Let it happen to me exactly as you say!"

Whooooosh! The angel and the whirlwind flew straight up into heaven and disappeared.

I was so happy then that I forgot about
the beans. I forgot about the hoe. I even forgot
about Joseph the carpenter, strong and true.

I raced to my mother and told her I was going on a
trip to visit cousin Elizabeth, and then I was gone.

Oh, I felt as if I were flying: south over a valley and over
the hills, south to the house of Zechariah, the husband of
Elizabeth.

Just as I was coming up the path, Elizabeth
stepped outside, wiping her hands on a towel.

"Hello!" I cried. "Hello, hello!"

As soon as she saw me, she dropped the towel
and grabbed her big stomach and gasped.

"Are you hurt?" I shouted. "Elizabeth, did
something hurt you?"

But my old, wrinkled cousin only started to
laugh. She ran to meet me and hugged me and put
wet kisses all over my face.

"No, I'm not hurt," she laughed. "When you
called out, my baby jumped for joy inside of me. Oh,
Mary, you are blessed among all the women of the
world, and blessed is your baby too."

Well, if Elizabeth was laughing, I laughed harder.
I laughed for gladness. I laughed for loving you
already, Yeshi. I laughed because
of the love of God.

And then, just like the angel, I sang a song about that love.
Do you want to hear my song? Okay. But close your eyes first.
It's getting late, and this is enough of the story tonight.

I sing the greatness of my God
Who chose to raise his lowly maid
While putting down the rich and proud:
Oh, holy is his name!
The Lord remembers Israel;
His mercy and his love remain;
As with our fathers it was well,
With us be it the same.

Good night, Yeshi. Good night, my beautiful child. The next
time we talk about your birthday, I'll tell you a secret—how
Joseph almost didn't become your daddy.

2

"**Yeshi!** It's time to come in."

Mary is calling through the window lattice to her son, who is still outside in the night. The straw mattress is already unrolled.

"Yeshi, come!"

The room they sleep in is also the room she cooks in. Her small clay stove sits in the far corner, together with three copper cooking pots, four earthen bowls, two water jars, and seven goatskin bags filled with grain and lentils and salt and spices. When they eat, they sit on the floor at a nice round mat.

"Ah, Yeshi, look at you!" Mary cries as Jesus enters the room.

His hair is tangled. He's covered in dust. His bandage is dirty and loose. Mary unties the bandage altogether.

"Oh, no!" she whispers.

The wound is an angry red, infected. Yellow pus runs from the corners.

"Sit down," Mary says. She goes to a pot of warm water and mixes salt into it.
She returns with the water and a rag and a jar of medicine, and sits down
beside her son.

"I have to wash it," she says. "I'm sorry, Yeshi, but when I wash
it, it will burn. The burning is the healing. Hush, hush," says
Mary. She puts her left arm around her son. With her
right hand she begins to wash his face, his forehead,
and his terrible wound.

"Ow!" Jesus gasps. His eyes go very
wide, then the tears come into

them and start to run down his dirty cheeks. "Oooooo."

"I know, I know," his mother murmurs. "But it must come clean."

Soon Mary is smearing medicine on his clean wound, an ointment made from animal fat and lint and honey. Honey kills germs. No bandage this time.

Softly Jesus is crying.

So Mary gathers him into her arms and rocks him, back and forth, back and forth.

"I love you, my son. Just as I told you in the story last night, I loved you from the very beginning.

"Tonight I'll tell you about someone else who loved you even before you were born. You see, your adopted daddy *almost* didn't marry me!"

Joseph's Love

I decided to stay with my cousin Elizabeth until her baby was born. That was a long time—about three months.

And all the while that I was gone, I missed Joseph the carpenter, strong and true. We were engaged to be married. We were *betrothed*, Yeshi—a very serious thing to be. It's the same as marriage, except that we weren't living in the same house yet.

Eight days after Elizabeth's baby was born, I started to travel home to Nazareth. The little life in my stomach slowed me down, but I felt so happy and so excited, because I had such wonderful news to tell Joseph.

As soon as I was back in Nazareth, I rushed over to Joseph's house and knocked on the door.

"Joseph, Joseph, come out!" I called. "Wait till I tell you what God is doing for us!"

The door opened up and there was Joseph, big as a bear, grinning and nodding and spreading his arms. I ran straight into those arms, and he hugged me with his wonderful strength.

Suddenly he stepped back and patted me on my stomach.

"Mary," he said, "you're getting fat."

"Yes," I said, "isn't that wonderful?"

Joseph frowned, puzzled. "It's *good* to be fat?" he said.

"Well," I said, "there's a good *reason* why I'm fat, a little tiny reason deep down inside of me."

Joseph frowned harder. "Mary, is this a riddle?"

I giggled and giggled and pinched his big nose. "It's better than a riddle." I laughed. "It's a living thing. Yesterday, Joseph, I felt that little tiny reason wiggle in my stomach."

"Wiggle?" Joseph said. "How can a reason wiggle?"

"Oh, Joseph," I shouted, "it's a baby! I'm going to have a baby!"

"A baby?" he said.

"Yes! This is what God is doing for us—a baby!"

I put out my arms so that he could hug me again, but he didn't. Joseph's frown grew darker and darker, like the cloud.

"This is impossible," he said, "unless … unless …"

"It's a baby straight from God," I said. "Won't you hug me, Joseph?"

He lowered his head. He didn't look at me. His frown got so hard that it broke, and only sadness was left. I saw tears running from his eyes.

"Joseph, please hug me," I said. "Oh, Joseph, hug me again."

But he turned away from me. He went into his house and shut the door, and I was left alone.

It wasn't his baby, you see. He thought it belonged to another man. But we were *betrothed!* If I was having a baby by another man, then this was a wicked sin!

"Joseph, I didn't sin!" I shouted through the door. "Truly, I did not sin against God, and I did not sin against you!"

He didn't answer me. He didn't say anything. He didn't come out again.

Finally, I went to my own house and fell on my bed and burst into tears. All day long I cried.

Joseph is a good man, strong and true. He always obeys the laws of God. And because he thought that I had sinned, I knew exactly what he was planning to do.

He was going to divorce me and never see me again. That's why I was crying so hard.

That night my mother brought me some soup, but I told her I wasn't hungry and to leave me alone.

Early the next morning my father came into my room and said, "You haven't slept all night."

I said, "Leave me alone."

He said, "Should I tell Joseph to leave you alone too?"

"Joseph?" I whispered. "Is *Joseph* here?"

"Yes, just outside the door."

I jumped up and rushed outside, and there he was. There was my own dear Joseph, big as a bear. He wasn't frowning any more, so I went to him and, yes, he hugged me so hard that we both started crying together.

He said, "I was going to divorce you."

I said, "I know."

He said, "But last night the angel of the Lord came to me in my sleep and told me that your baby is from God. He said we should name the baby Jesus."

"Jesus," I whispered. "That's exactly what the angel told me too. Oh, Joseph, I was so lonely. I thought you were never coming back to me."

"Well," he said, "the *real* reason why I came is … is to ask: will you go home with me? Right now? Mary, I want you to be my wife starting now and lasting as long as we both live."

Oh, how the birds sang in the sky that day, while I went home with my new husband, Joseph the carpenter, strong and true.

You see, Yeshi? Six months before you were born, a good man promised to love you as much as I do—your adopted daddy, Joseph.

Now *he* has traveled south over a valley and over the hills, south to the house of my cousin Elizabeth. He's building her a whole new roof. It's a hard job. It takes a long time to make someone's house warm and dry. But he will come home when he is done, Yeshi, to keep our house warm and dry. And maybe he'll bring you a gift when he does. Maybe.

Does your forehead sting now? No? I'm glad. Salt is the healing hurt. Sleep, my child, sleep tonight—and soon I will tell you the very best part of your birthday story.

3

When Mary comes into the room on this night, Jesus is already lying on the straw mattress with his eyes squeezed shut.

Mary whispers, "Is my baby sleeping?"

The boy makes a tiny giggle, but he squeezes his eyes even tighter.

"Yes, yes, my son is sleeping," Mary whispers.

Jesus giggles. His face grows pink.

"What a good boy!" his mother says. "Oh, how proud I am of the child who goes to sleep so early and all on his own!"

By now the wound on Jesus' forehead has turned into a solid brown scab, good protection for the healing. And it's itchy. With his eyes scrunched closed, he reaches up as fast as a fly and scratches the scab.

"Well, I guess I better go," Mary says. "I wanted to tell Yeshi the absolute best part of his birth story, but since he's already sleeping, it's too late—"

"Mommy! Mommy, *wait!*"

Jesus shoots up from the mattress and almost knocks his mother over.

"Oh, Yeshi!" Mary laughs, "you woke up so fast! Were you having a dream?"

She kisses his itchy scar and then lies down on the mattress with him, both heads on the goat-hair pillow.

"Okay," Mary says, "I told you about my love and Joseph's love, about how the angel came first to me and then to your adopted daddy. Now comes the best love in all the world—and this time, Yeshi, the angels come on account of *you!*"

God's Love

Six months after we were married, Joseph the carpenter, strong and true, strapped a cloth saddle to the back of our donkey. Then he lifted me up and put me on that saddle, and then he started to lead the donkey south. We walked one day and two days and three days.

Joseph had to be strong to lift me up, Yeshi. You were as big as a watermelon inside of me. Sometimes you kicked so hard that you made lumps poke out of my stomach. Oh, you were ready to be born, all right—and I was very, very tired.

But we *had* to go to Bethlehem. That's the town where your great-great-great-grandaddy was born: David, the king of Israel. All the people in the empire had to go to the cities of their great-grandaddies, you see, so that we could be counted for the official records.

Well, just after sunset on the third day of traveling, we came to the little town of Bethlehem. I was so tired and so sore, and now it was getting dark. There were hundreds and hundreds of strangers walking up and down the roads, and no one said hello to us.

Joseph led the donkey to a low stone house and knocked. When a woman opened the door, he said, "Do you have a place where my wife and I can lie down for the night?"

The woman swung the door wide open, and we could see that mattresses had already been unrolled over every inch of floor.

"No," she said.

She shut the door—

—and suddenly I screamed at the top of my lungs, with all my might: "*JO-O-O-SEPH!*"

He rushed over to me, shouting, "What's the matter?"

I had such a big pain in my stomach that I could scarcely talk. "The baby is coming!" I croaked. "The baby wants to be born *right now!*"

Poor Joseph! He started knocking on the doors of every house in sight.

Knock, knock!

"Do you have room for me and my wife?"

"No, no room here."

Knock, knock, knock!

"My wife is having a baby. Do you—"

"Nope! Nothing!"

I hollered: "Hurry, Joseph! Hurry! Hurry!"

Knock, knock!

"My wife needs somewhere to lie down—"

"Go away! We don't want any beggars here!"

"Please help us!"

"Go away!"

By now the night was pitch black. All the muscles in my stomach were pushing, pushing, trying to make the baby come. I tried not to scream again, but I couldn't help it. I opened up my mouth and released a scream as bright as a burning arrow: *"JOSEPH, WE CAN'T WAIT ANY MORE!"*

Right away he was at my side. He had a wild look in his eyes.

He cried, "Mary, I know where to go!" Then he led the donkey quickly to the last house in the city, around to the back of that house, and down to a small cave where travelers tether their animals overnight.

"Here!" he shouted, and in we went.

He lit an oil lamp.

I saw the faces of the animals, watching us. Even the birds woke up to watch.

Joseph lifted me down and lay me on some clean straw.

I said, "Lord, Lord, come help me now!" And I pushed. Oh, Yeshi, how I pushed! I pushed so hard, I could have moved a boulder uphill—and suddenly, there you were!

Little tiny baby, so beautiful in your face, you made a wonderful squawk to prove you were alive, and I loved you!

I washed you, Jesus. And I rubbed you with salt till your skin grew bright. And I kissed you. And I wrapped you in strips of clean cloth from your chest to your toes. And I laid you in a manger, and you grinned at me, and I laughed for joy, and all the animals watched, and the little birds sang, and Joseph the carpenter, strong and true, brought some water for me and two kisses for you.

We loved you, Yeshi, both of us.

But someone loved you
even more than we did.
God in heaven loved you.
And how do I know?
Because of the angels who came to sing.
You see, that night there were shepherds watching their
sheep in a valley outside of Bethlehem.

At the very moment you were born, they saw a bolt of lightning
drop from heaven and hit the hill in front of them. It was an angel. It was
the angel of the Lord, and the shepherds fell flat in the grass and covered
their eyes.

"No," said the angel, "don't be afraid. I'm bringing you good news,
joyful news, news for *all* the people! Listen: this very night in Bethlehem a
baby has been born—a baby now, a Savior forever! And who do you think
he is? Why, he is Christ the Lord!"

The shepherds started to peep up at the angel.

The angel grinned. "And this is how you can find him," he said.
"He's wrapped in strips of clean cloth and lying in a manger."

One by one the shepherds stood up. Then, suddenly, all
the stars of the night started to move! They streaked through
the darkness like comets. They whirled closer and closer to
the earth—and just as the shepherds saw that the stars were
angels, well, the angels burst into a beautiful chorus:

Glory, glory!
Glory to God in the highest of high!
And on earth peace—
Peace to the people with whom he is pleased!

Yeshi, I heard the star-angels sing. And almost as soon as their song was done, here came those shepherds running to our little cave. They came to see you. They gazed at you with shining eyes of gladness and of awe.

A woman shepherd leaned forward and kissed you in the middle of your forehead. You opened your eyes and looked at her, and she covered her mouth. That shepherd, she wept tears of pure joy.

Do you see how strong for you was the love of God? It filled the humble people too, and when they went out into the night, I could hear them singing just like the angels, singing glory to God on account of you.

Go to sleep, my child. Go to sleep now, Jesus. I kiss you too, in the middle of your forehead. I kiss the hurt that the stone's throw gave you. I kiss the pain and the itching away—for a little while. A little while.

When the time is right, I must tell you one more part of the birthday story, the part that taught me why you were born and why you came into this world.

Good night, my child. Sleep tight while you can, before you become a man.

Good night.

Mary has a mirror made of polished bronze. Once when Joseph built a table for a woman who had no money, she gave him the mirror as payment, and he gave it to his wife.

Mary keeps it in a cloth pouch and almost never uses it. Why should she? She doesn't paint her eyes or braid her hair or rub red rouge on her cheeks. And she'd rather look at her husband or her boy, not at herself.

How surprised she is, then, to find the cloth pouch empty and the mirror missing.

Who needs her mirror?

It's dark outside. Did someone come and steal it?

Joseph has been gone to Elizabeth's house for a long time, now—but he never looks at himself in a mirror.

Suddenly Mary notices a flicker of light under the door of a small storage room.

Softly she opens that door, and there is Jesus squatting beside an oil lamp, staring down at his reflection in Mary's mirror.

He is very serious.

He has picked the scab away from his forehead and is gazing at the new skin beneath. Jesus has a shining scar. It is in the shape of two crooked lines, one crossing the other.

Mary kneels beside him and puts her arm around him and says, "That scar will be with you all your life long, Yeshi. Some things never go away."

Mary takes her son into her arms and kisses the scar on his forehead.

"The angel told us to name you *Jesus*," she whispers in his ear, "and so we did, eight days after you were born. But the angel also told us what that name means, and now it's time for you to know the meaning because it explains what you will do when you grow up. Yeshi, *Jesus* means: *He will save his people from their sins.*"

Mary picks up the mirror and stares at her son's reflection there. His face is a rich brown color in the bronze.

"About a month after you were born," she says, "a very old man named Simeon made a prophecy about your future. He said that you would shine God's light of love in all the world, and that's a good thing. He said that you were going to be the salvation of every nation everywhere, a very good thing!

"But then he said that you would be like a stone, and people would stub their toes against you, and fall down because of you, and blame you, and hate you. Oh, Yeshi! That is *not* good. That makes me very sad."

Mary puts the mirror down and hugs her child. There are tears in her eyes.

"Such hard things to come," she whispers. "Simeon said that it would feel like a sword going through my soul.

"Come. Lie down. You are old enough now to hear the last part of your birth story. There is love for you in this part too, from wise men and from strangers. But there is also danger and hatred. After old Simeon talked to us, Yeshi, I learned that the greatest loving in your life will not be the love that comes *to* you. No, it will be the love that goes out *from* you to the whole wide world. That, dear Jesus, is the real meaning of your name."

Your Love for All the World

Joseph and I found a little house in Bethlehem where we lived for several years. During that time you learned to crawl and then to walk.

And very soon you learned to talk.

Abba! you said. Your first words were *Abba,* father.

Oh, Yeshi, you ran and laughed in the sunlight like any child. You smeared your face with fresh grapes. The birds seemed to laugh at the sight of you. And wherever your adopted daddy carried his toolbox, you followed, chattering like the sparrows.

Life was so happy in Bethlehem that we thought we might stay there forever. But then the danger came, and we had to leave suddenly, in the middle of the night.

Here's how it started.

One afternoon you ran into the house with your eyes as round as millstones.

"Doggies! Big doggies!" you shouted. You threw your arms wide open and shouted, "Horsies! *Elephunks!*"

You raced outside. You raced in again, shouting, "Mommy, come out. Men are here on *elephunks!*"

I stepped to the door and saw your elephunks. But I didn't laugh. I held my breath at the wonder of the scene before me.

There were camels come to our little house—and on the camels, men who had traveled hundreds and hundreds of miles across the desert from foreign lands to Bethlehem.

"What—" I said, "—what do you want?"

"We have come," they said, "to worship the one who has been born king of the Jews."

"But there's no king here," I said, "just a carpenter and his poor family."

"No, you are wrong," said one of them, an old man with a long white beard. "Look," he said, and he pointed to the sky. I came out and looked up and saw a bright star in the daylight sky—right over our little house!

"We are called Magi, Wise Men," said the second foreigner, young and ruddy and beardless. "We can read the stars as if they were words on a page. And *that* star says that the child who lives in this house is the king we are seeking."

You, Yeshi! They had come to see you.

The third man was an African with a heavy beard. He said, "The old king, Herod, told us to look in Bethlehem. He invited us into his palace and told us that the Christ was supposed to be born here—and then he smiled, and he asked us to come back and tell him how to find the child himself. He said he wanted to worship the new king, too."

Yeshi, you were not even two years old. But after the Wise Men said these things I saw you change. All at once you seemed to be a thousand years old! You walked into the house. You sat down with your back to the wall and folded your arms and waited for the Magi to come to you.

I said in my soul, *Who is this child?*

One by one the men came in. One by one they kneeled down before you. One by one they placed gifts at your feet: gold and frankincense and myrrh. And I shuddered, because gold belongs to kings, and frankincense is given to God, and myrrh is what we put on the people we love when they die.

Oh, Yeshi, such a glorious future was laid out before you then! And the worship of the Wise Men was as if the whole world had come to know you and to honor you.

That night the foreigners stayed with us in our humble house.

After supper we all lay down to sleep, Joseph and you and I in one room, the three visitors in another.

In the middle of the night, two men started to groan. Their groanings grew louder and louder, frightening me.

One was the African Magi. I couldn't help *him*, but the other man was your adopted daddy, so I shook him and shook him until he woke up, and then he went to wake the other man too.

Well, they both had been dreaming dreams.

The African's dream warned him never to go back to King Herod. All the Wise Men should travel home by a different route.

And in your daddy's dream the angel of the Lord said that we should run away as fast as we could. He said to flee to Egypt, because old King Herod wanted to kill you, Yeshi.

So we all left.

The Magi went east on their camels, and we went south on a donkey.

And then this is the news we heard: in seven days King Herod became an angry man, a crazy man.

"Where are the Magi?" he yelled. "Why aren't they coming back to me? If they don't tell me where the baby king lives, how can I find him to kill him?"

The king stuck his head out a palace window and roared his horrible orders: "I am the king of the Jews! No one should be king except me—never, never! Soldiers, go down to Bethlehem and kill every boy-child who is less than two years old!"

Even in Egypt we learned of this sin. Even in Egypt we heard the sad wailing of all the mothers who had lost their little boys.

But soon the angel came to see us for the last time, bringing the news that set us free.

"Terrible King Herod is dead," the angel said, "and now he isn't the king of anything."

The angel gazed at us with his marvelous eyes and spoke with a voice as gentle as breezes in the cedar trees:

"Go home," he said. "Take your child back to Nazareth and raise him there to be both strong and wise—and he shall be precious to God forever."

Mary pulls the woolen blanket up to the chin of her child.

"That's it," she whispers. "That's your story. It is happy and it is sad. There is danger in the world, Yeshi, and hatred and sin, and when you grow up these things will hurt you."

Mary touches the tip of her finger to the scar on Jesus' brow. Then she leans down and touches her forehead to his.

"But when you grow up," she murmurs, "you will be the one to heal the dangers and hatred and sin of the world. One day all the children will know you, Yeshi. They will hear your birthday story, and they will be happy, because you loved them, every one, according to the meaning of your name, *Jesus*: you loved them enough to save them from their sins."

Suddenly there is a great banging outside the house, a booming and a stomping.

Mary and Jesus both turn to stare at the door.

It flies open and there, filling the doorframe with his big shoulders and an even bigger grin, is Joseph the Carpenter, strong and true!

"Daddy!" Jesus cries, flying from his bed to his father's arms. "Daddy, Daddy, you're home!"

Mary watches, smiling quietly, as Joseph lifts Yeshi high in the air.

"Home again—oh, yes I am!" Joseph roars. "And I have brought gifts for my boy, because he's growing up so fast. Sit, Yeshi, sit. It's time I taught you the work that I do."

Joseph winks at Mary. She nods. They have talked about this moment.

So the father of Jesus brings a leather bag inside the house. He, too, sits—face to face with his family—then gives his son new tools: a hammer, a saw, a chisel, some nails, and two fresh wooden boards.

"Smell the wood," Joseph says.

Jesus does and smiles because of its sweetness.

Joseph says, "Put one board on top of the other." And Jesus does that, too.

"Good, Yeshi. That's perfect. Now, then—take your hammer and just one nail, and make the boards stay like that forever."

So Jesus bends forward, frowning over his task, and begins to hammer the very first nail of all his life.

Mary watches while Joseph teaches Jesus his trade. But Mary isn't the only one.

The angels are watching.

And God the Father in heaven is leaning low to see.

And all the world is waiting, the shepherds and you and me.